PENGUIN BOOKS
Scenes From Comus

GEOFFREY HILL

Born in Bromsgrove, Worcestershire, in 1932, Geoffrey Hill is the author of three books of criticism and ten books of poetry, including *The Triumph of Love*, co-winner of the Heinemann Award. His *Collected Poems, Canaan, The Triumph of Love, Speech! Speech!, The Orchards of Syon* and *Scenes from Comus* are all published by Penguin.

Geoffrey Hill currently lives and teaches in Massachusetts, where he is Professor of Literature and Religion at Boston University. He is also Honorary Fellow of Keble College, Oxford; Honorary Fellow of Emmanuel College, Cambridge; Fellow of the Royal Society of Literature; and since 1996 Fellow of the American Academy of Arts and Sciences.

Scenes From Comus

GEOFFREY HILL

PENGUIN BOOKS

PENGUIN BOOKS

Published by the Penguin Group
Penguin Books Ltd, 80 Strand, London WC2R ORL, England
Penguin Group (USA), Inc., 375 Hudson Street, New York, New York 10014, USA
Penguin Books Australia Ltd, 250 Camberwell Road,
Camberwell, Victoria 3124, Australia
Penguin Books Canada Ltd, 10 Alcorn Avenue, Toronto, Ontario, Canada M4V 3B2
Penguin Books India (P) Ltd, 11 Community Centre,
Panchsheel Park, New Delhi – 110 017, India
Penguin Group (NZ), cnr Airborne and Rosedale Roads, Albany,
Auckland 1310, New Zealand
Penguin Books (South Africa) (Pty) Ltd, 24 Sturdee Avenue,
Rosebank 2196, South Africa

Penguin Books Ltd, Registered Offices: 80 Strand, London WC2R ORL, England

www.penguin.com

Published in Penguin Books 2005
1

Set in 11/14.25 pt Aldus
Typeset by Rowland Phototypesetting Ltd, Bury St Edmunds, Suffolk

Printed in England by Clays Ltd, St Ives plc

FOR HUGH WOOD
ON HIS 70TH BIRTHDAY

> Who knows not *Circe*
> The daughter of the Sun?
> – John Milton

> The good walk in step. Without knowing anything of
> them, the others dance around them, dancing the dances
> of the age.
> – Franz Kafka

> VERY WELL ACTED BY YOU AND ME.
> – Wyndham Lewis

(1)

The Argument of the Masque

1

Of the personality as a mask;
of character as self-founded, self-founding;
and of *the sacredness of the person*.

Of licence and exorbitance, of scheme
and fidelity; of custom and want of custom;
of dissimulation; of envy

and detraction. Of *bare preservation*,
of *obligation to mutual love*;
and of our covenants with language

contra tyrannos.

2

That we are inordinate creatures
not so ordained by God; that we are
at once rational, irrational – and there is reason.

That this is no reason for us to despair.
The tragedy of things is not conclusive;
rather, one way by which the spirit moves.

That it moves in circles need not detain us.
Marvel at our contrary orbits. Mine
salutes yours, whenever we pass or cross,

which may be now, might very well be now.

3

Titagrams work: balls-ache at the threshold.
Mute apathy not now in order, try
provoking our old selves mono-duet.

Say, thirty years until H. M. commands
a small obstruction for the mantelpiece
and senna's called on more than single malt.

Inspiration breathes hard. Still your music
would arouse Milton fór me, if he required
such service óf us. He doesn't, does he?

Let's go to ground around the grinning cake.

4

Language of occasion has here fallen
into occurrence of outcry, reactive
outcry, like a treatable depression

that happens not to respond. If fate,
then fated like autism. There is some notion,
here, of the sea guffawing off reefs,

to which we compose our daft music
of comprehension. Rain-front on rain-front,
then a sun-gash, clouds moody; the sea's mood

turns from slate-black, to yellow ochre, to green.

5

Add that we're unaccountably | held to account;
that we cannot make our short days add up
to the sum demanded. Add, that accountancy

is a chartered profession, like surveying;
that rectitude is a grand directive;
that righteousness has no known charter

and is not, generally speaking, in demand.
That there are immoderate measures in plenty;
that plenty is a term of moderation;

that moderation is by some used to excess.

6

That, in these latter days, language
is the energy of decaying sense;
that sense in this sense means *sensus communis*.

That common sense bids me add: not
all language. If power's fuelled by decay,
so be it – decay being a natural force.

Moral corruption is another matter;
I cannot get beyond pronouncing it
inertia of malevolence, or *pondus*.

This *pondus* has itself nothing to add.

7

That stale enlightenment exacerbates
the incoherence – ask me to explain –
profuse expediency that leaves us speechless,

wordless, even. Their words attack my throat
wordlessly. If it were silence to silence!
Silence is shown defending a loved child

against | incorrigible fact. Mute
suffering's a factor of countless decibels.
I see the pristine hammer hammer alarm.

I see it but I can hear nothing.

8

That the imagination is a type
of reactor. Mine works well with bursts
of winter-sun chill-out in Reykjavik,

orgiastic shuteye. A critical mass:
impression into expression. Where's the many
times caught and expelled, all-sufficient child,

transfigured memory, now that the sun's gone in?
*The Monad begetteth the Monad, and doth
reflect upon itself its own fervour.*

The man who said this died of alchemy.

9

Draw together the surviving powers,
the *dark Aleph* and the *Father of Lights*.
I imagine them majestic in winter,

though not as they used to be still dangerous.
I say imagine them I mean create them –
another remnant of alchemical twaddle

that ceases to be twaddle in some cases,
and in some degrees, of allayed loathing.
Any fire to transmute these fraudulent base years!

I say create them I mean imagine them.

10

That the receptor and reactor are a unit
making themselves many units of energy;
that the voice of prophecy clings to its logged spar;

that the deep waters toss me about – I shout
from the crests and the troughs, these words that turn
to a spooled marker-dye the colour of vomit;

even so cannot cease from invoking the sea's
unchallengeable voltage, its transforming waste.
The need for good reactors I also accept –

the alchemy ∣ the primal infiltration.

11

Sexual love – instinctively alchemical:
early sexual love. Or is the dying
recreation of it the real mystery?

I say that each is true: words troth-plight
to both of us, equal with her, truer
now, than I wás or ever could be,

but knowing myself in her. I said
ask me to explain – they won't remember,
forty-six lines back and already buried

with the short day.

12

That *marriage is a hieroglyphic*, stands
in its own garment. Not a possession.
Not always dispossessed. Or to speak

otherwise: it brings ruin and the numen
together; and indeed it cán
be a lovely thing when others make it so.

That numen, too, is a hieroglyph –
a shadow brought to bear, a signal.
And that reason is articulate in the will

if you don't think about it.

13

That I mean what I say | saying it obscurely.
I would lie to anyone in all frankness.
Rhetoric is weaponry, should not be allowed

to fiddle the equation. We are a hand's span
from the end of time. Milton thought so
and rejoiced in so thinking. Perhaps

he was right, perhaps it has been and gone,
sudden death trumpets, Armageddon, the taking
up of the elect, their inurement, the totalled

compact reality of all evil fictions.

14

Not in these noises – Milton. *A troubled sea
of noises and hoarse disputes*, is also him.
Even short arctic days have a long twilight

as I have time to observe. Gloam lies pulsing
at the sea-skyline, where the *Hood* blew up
surging at full speed, a kind of wake

over the sudden mass grave foul with cordite,
gradually settling. Milton meant civil war
and civil detractions, and the sway of power,

the pull of power, its *pondus*, its gravity.

15

Somewhere I have lost *Milton on Music*
and *The English Masque*. Sometime in the last days.
I thought they were in the bag. Three gross men

and three skeletal women mouth me
the world's disasters. Milton would have laughed.
Save these for the antimasque. The antimasque

will not be saved, not from the winter sea,
the *stormy Hebrides*. My spirit salutes yours
unclaimed. To reduce is to lead back,

to rectify; also, to diminish.

16

That the antimasque is what saves us
challenge by challenge. Still I anticipate.
I did not anticipate the marriage

that I destroyed. It was not then the fashion.
The Ludlow Masque was far from fashionable
though fashioned well. To up the bid, superbly.

Milton's *superbia* is a joy to hear:
triumphal reticence, verse to be delivered
badly and to survive; and this by virtue

of Comus' gifts – not meant to be so taken.

17

That actors think too highly of themselves.
O damn this *pondus* of splenetic pride!
Sleet's always driven sideways in my experience;

hard at it now, rustles like harsh tissue
or creaks against the glass. As Milton said,
no more chiding. He had some years to go.

Someone had to forgive him. No, not himself.
His daughters, maybe, though that story's garbled.
He was a cheerful soul and loved your music,

Hugh, as he must have told you many times.

18

I'm wresting myself into simplicity –
exhaustion's bonanza – also I want to leave
something in trust, something by definition

not by default. Head-on the big crows
halt the wind, the gulls plane in wide curves,
vanishing among the flurries; fields are blue-brown

with a top-dressing of snow. In whose name
such conflagrations of undeeded gifts?
If not Milton then Hardy; if not

Hardy, Lawrence – *Look! We Have Come Through!*

19

That from this noise, this mêlée, there issues
a grand and crabby music. And that I
want my piece of it. Even when not mine.

That vows so made are like lights on snow-ploughs,
purpose and power at once. Look what gets
tossed aside. Massive effects are junked.

And they talk about Heavy Metal! They don't know,
these kids, what weight of the word is,
that in the half dark of commodity most

offers are impositions.

20

That weight of the world, weight of the word, is.
Not wholly irreconcilable. Almost.
Almost we cannot pull free; almost we escape

the leadenness of things. Almost I have walked
the first step upon water. Nothing beyond.
The inconceivable is a basic service.

Hyphens are not-necessary for things I say.
Nor do I put to strain their erudition –
I mean, the learned readers of J. Milton.

But weight of the world, weight of the word, is.

(2)

Courtly Masquing Dances
nello stile antico

1

Weight of the world, weight of the word, is.
Take it slowly, like walking
through convalescence, the load
bearing not yet adjusted, progress
made with a slight forward and sideways tilt,
or otherways angled, one hip
acting up, strung on a wire.
How heartening it is when it goes right –
the moment of equipollence, a signal.

2

Indebtedness is resolved by paying debts,
strangely enough; justice, not metaphysics;
custom, restitution, setting to rights and rest.
Law-breaking too is in the hierarchy,
and riding westward, post-haste. This
brings us to Michaelmas, its rule and riot,
its light a fading nimbus over Wales.

3

The river the forest, the river ís the forest,
the forest the ríver, swamps of loosestrife
choking fecundity. Sabrina, she also, chaste
genius of teeming and dying,
I fancy her
trailing labiles, placentas, uncomely swags.
My own lines double here as her lianas.

4

The time of our sleeping, that is beyond time
in the author's progress. Are you convinced by sleep?
At some level I ám, though still forgetful.
You appear largely in possession, Sabrina;
your waters never sleep – now kept in spate
by Cambrian readjustments far up-stream;
your stretch of the interminable
journey to closure
that gathers beauty, tearing as it goes.

5

Inducted by Marvell I have brought along
my *wanton troopers* – squaddies, as we know them.
I watch them urging throúgh, at some low ford,
their rowels nicking. Fawns? There áre fawns,
even nów, ín the still haunted purlieus
between Bewdley and Ludlow; and stags rutting.
Of the sexual lives of children I speak elsewhere.
And of white wood-sorrel long called *alleluia*.
And of the rut of begetting.

6

Masques are booked to be simple, sensuous,
comely, shaped to a fair design;
not over-passionate;
free from dark places and equivocation,
present a tidy challenge, less to the maker
than to the persons in the entertainment,
young noble clones safely beset by clowns.

7

This our egregious masking – what it entails.
Our sex-masques plague-threatened. Our murrain'd
rustic to-and-fro-ing, lording it here, and there,
craven in vanity. I mean, lawful
lordship, powers that múst be, I do not grudge.
Nor do I challenge the power of the Lord
President in Cymru. *Diolch – diolch yn fawr!*

8

I doubt Marvell bought out ǀ Milton's fouled life.
But bring on music, sonorous, releasing.
What we háve becomes their reticence.
Within the radius of a storm's hollow
like honey in a tree. Bayed Milton reticent?
Or that wit-bibber from Hull? I say self-being
goes the last word with bóth, that it goes proud
in its own passion – mystical couvade
with sensual dying, sensuous rebirth.

9

Suppose, ingenious, we tell our loves
haemony's in the script, melts like a pearl,
chemical self-renewal not to be paid for,
retroactively inheres, working forgiveness
within the act, enriches all performance
in the great masquing- or presence-chamber
of reason and desire:
you with your daemon or genius, I with one
who for the fiction's sake must feel betrayed.

10

Suppose I tell it otherwise: haemony
is of the blood (therefore the lovely name);
the elect possess it, subject to possession;
it cannot be bought, bartered, part exchanged.
The sun is drawn away, darkness advances
bleeding our scene, mysterious dry ice
tinctured with earth-smoke, Orphic harbinger.

11

Its prickliness is infamous – famous,
so many contesting – dim prodigy
uncultivated
and of glummest fruition.
Proffer it then to that transparent virgin
of pregnant chastity;
let her go | far afflicted with her friends.

12

Haemony may mean technē | now he tells me.
Haemony means whatever Milton | meánt by it.
Wisdom of the blood | was not intended.
He was his own | man, like Lawrence. Not
proto anything | that I can think of.
Nor was Lawrence blood | wisdom in isolation.
Look at our tangled | history. Neptune's
forest submerging | compounding its coal measures,
smoke-enriched England | her children ashen.

13

Yes, Comus, about time – about time
and justification. That's beginning
to match a laggard forwardness. In touch,
my other self – so held – once it's too late;
my other pulse, beating to Plato's rhythm
heard through circadian circuits of distress.
Loud hissing in the ears may or may nót
mean blood pressure soaring, or sex on heat,
or siren voices, or yr lisping snakes.

14

I've not pieced out the story – Milton's script
was briefly censored, bits of sex expunged
for the girl's sake. Chastity makes its bed
with sensuality, could not otherwise
use such authoritative vehemence
devoid of knowingness.
It's an attractive doctrine to me now.

15

Hereditary thresholds, I recognize
how often you're mysterious disenchanters,
enablers of some journeys but not this
where England ends half way across a field,
the valley of the Honddu at the cleft
church of Cwm Yoy, its displaced gravity;
and I not moving and yet moving on.

16

The red sandstone forest, fern-shouldering streams;
the Severn also, cliff-cutting, wide-wading,
the commonness of the prodigious journey –
no memory of those lóst prínces who wait
to be dúg úp by Grimm – the words of un-
expected and expected salutation;
the young commoner, Lawes's find, not found
at the scene of his making, who might now
be thought well worthy an earl's daughter.

17

Oh, and yes, Comus, báck to our vanity;
now I have brought you out, a shared advantage,
to walk and take the air around the moat –
though this smells bad tonight. So be my guest
emissary, or janissary, to the swans
who ride the higher air, when they've a mind,
mysterious radii, nót given to tread
with any flesh of spirit, ór be trodden
by any but the airiest incubi.

18

This is a fabled England, vivid
in winter bareness; bleakly comforting,
the faded orchard's hover of grey-green.
We have come home, say, all is well between us.
Sharp-shining berries bleb a thorn, as blood
beads on a finger or a dove's breast pierced
by an invisible arrow to the heart.

19

Too many of us. I have laid you
waste with such love.
But such waste as becomes fecundity
in the eyes of others: the sun strikes
through these dimensions, cumulus
burns tortoiseshell-umber, lanterned
from inside the mass.

20

To show immediately how it all works:
Platonic theology's flight simulators;
no call to leave the ground of our estate.
There are designs that light the empyrean.
I have in mind more I something like Great Tew's
model symposium that's set in motion
by slow airs fluted on the inlaid grass,
aubades to angels from the sons of earth.
The eternal round's a fixture on their screens.

21

He means the poets, and he has these moments.
Also he has his lines, the dying
swán that chánts, enchánted to the stream,
palmed off on you know who. They say the red-
tailed kite is back, inland from Aber,
in soaring numbers, some in the Thames Valley,
round Cuddesdon's small, declivitous plateau
where even the snails are different. And the birds.
Near where they set him up with Mary Powell.

22

Sharpened, sharpening, the swifts' wings
track and loop back clear skeins
through vanished arches.
See in what ways the river
lies padded – no, dashed – with light.
Show whether the imaged clouds
are litanies or escorts.

23

Tacitus described the Phoenix once,
mentioning myrrh and semen, which must mean fire.
Steady now, old heart, longevity
is not at all the Heraclitean thing.
See – hear – how sparks
fly from the burning-plumed rôtisserie –
painful the fable ardently re-wound.

24

Alongside these travesties stands my own
vision of right order. Some forms, orders,
travesty themselves. That is today's
communiqué. Tomorrow's communiqué
will read the same.
World-webbed collusions, clouded diplomacies,
are lightning when they strike and strike us down.
Of marriages I speak, as of right order
among the travesties.

25

It's not impossible to be the child
of Bacchus and Circe, all imagination,
a demon made against his deepest will
a choric figure awed by what he hears.
There ís a dogged beauty in the world,
unembarrassing goodness, honesty unfazed.
There's also the corrupter, the abuser,
the abused corrupted in accepted ways,
the ways of death, the deadliness of life.

26

The corrupter, the abuser, the liverish
ravager of domestic peace. The soi-disant
harmless eccentric. Nobody's harmless.
Neither is comedy. Maybe the polka
injured thousands. In this depleted time
revive me, take me to a blue
movie, hold my hand in the dark.

27

His storm is in our air; light-burdened leaves
electrify his keepings. Love appears
as though by being I named an equal self.
Reverse impulse, enjoy,
without collusion, your own
doubtful self-celebration; say no more.
Conclude, most things offload us with a glance.

28

Hard to imagine them so crámped: thírty
feet by síxty? – I can't believe it.
Were the first builders pinched for cash, or what?
Then thís thing – sudden – in the midst of them:
Comus, as we must call it, unconfined
disembarrassing itself of common vesture,
the hyphenated speech of titled actors,
the torches set like wild men on the walls
tossing swart-blooded fire.

29

Cán't have been torches in thát space; try
candelabra. Candles, torches and all, burn down
to their ugly sockets; and the castle:
a site of gaping sconces, puddled floors,
and sodden tidy grass with gleam of rime.
Need to think about this; if possible, not
wax portentous but not quip it away.
By ít he means yoú, Britannia, his 'deep
and passionate love', high-stepping into ruin.

30

Say that I ám gifted – and I'll touch you
for ordinary uncommon happiness. What
a weirdo, you think. Well, yes, I was wired weird.
Back to the forest, then, where still so much
is the matter of legend. I see us getting down
to something long since hallowed and nuptial,
nuptial or nothing, angrily desired.

31

These short ones are the sock-fillers. No,
do my life justice I now if anywhere,
register shock-survival, childhood
anaesthesia I like being sucked
down by the *Bismarck*, pressure, multi-
dimensional pain, dead sulphonamides
creaming the mastoid bone.

32

Knowledge does whát to sex or, as it comes,
consensual I word of conjure? Certainly
flesh has its own spirit but may not know that.
Would you call an experience with Donne's
Elegies providential? Where are tapers
tapers burning in the immortal vaults of love?
Who is this now approaching
love at first sight? And is excoriate
nót to cry from the heart?

33

Quiet – I'm still trying. Pity,
terror, you might care to empower them
as choruses, though they're as nothing
without judgement
of what instruments can do
to the human voice.
Imagine synthesizers
transforming the forest of our earth-drawn
metaphysical cries.

34

Die Fühlungsmühl – the hollow mill that turns
always full of itself. As master – briefly –
of my own skill, I call this to account
under a dated lintel, the gristing-chamber,
where for a lifetime it has ground me
an unnutritious powder, a black grain
against the grain of the stone.

35

Held by this half-literate grieving excitement,
honey-infused candles, this vigil: patriotism
is not unChristian; it's not Christian either,
I beg to plead. Transcendent indistinction
trashes the thought. Spirit bleeds everywhere
emoting body-pathos, not unlike
ectoplasm, or grease-paint from Hallowe'en.

36

It ejaculates its pain and is not
answered; nor acknowledged, even.
Give you these, by way of apology:
obvious things, patience that has for emblem
certain oblivious fibres, the flax-plant supremely;
chicory also, its sober chance provision;
the service tree, wíld, scárce, with healing willow;
the torchwort or mullein, as it is known,
and comfrey the waste-healer.

37

Harrowed three days, now Lazarus
breaking his fast. Dead Sickert's look-alike.
Post-flu invalid's diet and inappropriate
light-squinnied isolation. Abstemious wolfing,
loose-tied, flop hung, baggy, nappy-cravat,
big dish of mussels, stewed prunes, gleaming black stones,
spoon like a tongue-depresser ǀ gobbed straight in.
Poverty parodied – rich sensual man of parts –
death-grip on his revived inheritance.

38

And if by some such hazard something
incomparably finished, something beyond change
as by design ǀ yes, the great memory-surge
of raw beginning: snow-contoured strange Wildmoor
and our stiff ugly tasks; a single storm lamp
not thawing-out the frozen pipes; each pane
of the kitchen window quilted with white ferns.

39

Rewriting his own deepest reading: thát
fair comment on the wiped out fifty years
from genesis to this? Give me a break
in concentration, só I can concentrate,
as I once did – a Comus child – on pignuts,
on how the tree gum, malleable, came to hand
as damson-amber; which I tried to burn.

40

Go through it all again: Is this
the genius that approached you? Does it
have a name? Said I wísh I could draw you,
draw you so that you seem
not to be hiding, wísh I could draw you in?
Concede some kind of epic statement.
Sleep alone I fertile and barren friend.
Insulted witness of proven chastity.
Name of hotel?

41

All Saints | All Souls, the shades stay with the year;
and prayer has ratted ón me; and the leaves
have ratted on the boughs. November First,
variegate, attenuate, Japanese; high
spiritous colours, or wan, or putrid brown.
And I say: wátch – watch this phenomenon,
this other selving; it is yours to keep,
whose shadow reaches out, grows, is unhinged,
flung on the shattered pavement, breaks apart.

42

Read *me* throughout, the *du* is self reflexive
though not without exception. There are times
when I consort with music so to speak.
Speaking of which there's your reluctant gift – of
sorrow so prolific – and my own
fortune spent in mishearings; our voices pitched,
our minds of penury poised upon excess.

43

Their time not ours. They show it; are naked.
Name three still living awarded the Mons Star.
Love will not spare us the past. Old
men of seventy have nuisance value.
I snorkel into contrived sleep, I wake,
I address the mirror: *spare me my own
rancour and ugliness.* It too is naked.

44

I'm tired now the whole time and yet I wish to
take up my bed and walk:
to Compostela, for example,
bush-hat hung round with clamshells on return:
or ride the Gulf Stream through to Akureyri
and find a hot spring equal to my bulk
sheltered by palm trees, bowered by frangipani
or bougainvillia, wallowing in *Icelandic
Christian Poetry* till the fish come home.

45

Sprung from stacked cages racing-pigeons
with startling whurrawhurra
crowd to the air,
turning, co-radicate, radiate,
from this focus, the body
of their homing flight.
Where's the sun up to? I can see them
not now a wheel exactly, nor a fan,
more a silver bowl, the silver tarnishing.

46

The light – generous – discovers its ascent,
gives all it can bring us.
A haze, and at odd hours the moon also is there
appearing sea-worn.
But what a hope, the mild attrition
of a dove's call, the body
gradually winding down, becoming vacant.

47

The small oaks crest the ridge, the sun appears
cresting this instant. Their topmost ranks
take fire and vaporize
or find some other form wherewith to be
not of this world. How can I tell you? –
dawn after dawn, immeasurable taking up
of dross and dying.

48

Slouching at senescence. Whereas Ursa Minor
is the real McCoy, the true Cynosure:
whereas, what I believe I give you here
I take as the counterpoint to your own
caustic attrition and noble rest-
oration of music's power to console.
Whereas, thus, in proclaiming, in oration.
Seventeenth-century torch-songs did things well.
No slouches, then, whoever wrote them.

49

The stiff-eyed man in the colonial hat
directs his dotted eyebeams angled sharply
into the ground. Instantly they | re-
bound (from mirror or burnished metal)
these rays elliptical, soaring, crown
with hígh árt a solitary stunt pine.
Faith stands confirmed in trigonometry
keeping at nadir and at zenith, both,
its delphic zeal.

50

If this sleep mask is a time machine
a world attends us under a strange star,
our gifts are what we owe, each to the other,
and which we give: now there's no going back –
like *Wedding at the Marsh*, the true fiction
set in the one frame; or the book set down
marked at that page, not closed, and not returned to.

51

The ashen-purple soil looks ripe for winter,
as does the succubine ground ivy
snag-wrinkling over it. The wind veers
closer to silence than most things I know
outside your third quartet, music I
strain to catch
clamours of ⏐ diminution, abrupt rest.

52

Sei solo, a polished soundfocus, blunt splay fingers
unhasty, the bow attentive, now to be glimpsed
pistoning *tempo di bourrée*, and heard
clawing out four-string polyphony, a form
of high baritone *tessitura*,
groan, almost, and sighing – such depth – the instrument's
power from úpthrust, the return
equally measured: an athlete's kind of measure
with and against earth's torque and tricky camber.

53

Heady September heat with shadows thrown
across white walls. Sun – fetching us this instant!
Where áre we sans our lovers, yoú name the place?
The place itself is common; I have been here
many times and enough.
Love's grief is full, always popular,
like ghosted memoirs or the old
fashioned chara-tours,
like the Welsh hills covered in rhododendrons.

54

Absolutely all in all, all in the picture
exhibited to the jury | aged overnight.
Overnight seduction by a minor art
carries life, and the voyeur, with it
without any major recompense. The charge
is *anadiplosis* and the sentence
the sentence here handed down.

55

A fish-shaped embryo aureoled in flame
glows from the time-scarred retina's
scratch kaleidoscope. A thing even of beauty
I fancy – ánd less strange than goldfish
on black and white TV. Now Piscis breaks
out into floated plaques and warps of colour.
I'll join you – wobbly swimmers of the eye!

56

Restart from cold: crystallized
microchips on the plane window,
November Thirtieth; the pumice
and verdigris textured coastline of Iceland
steps up slowly as slowly we step down.
Can't tell you how unoften I accost
these graphic isolations. The swept-strewn
groundscape of Keflavik accommodates us,
I cán tell you.

57

Greetings *sul ponte*, fratello mio. If
careen means turning vessels on their side
to claw off barnacles; and if *fulsome*'s
the ríght word for befouling praise;
if the self servers now in full career –
against whóm you stood
and stand no chance, none, stop
scratching and sighing – and if *cól*
légno means whácking it with báck of bów –

58

Feed the seven cats, pray to the household gods.
Try on the new Timon of Athens face.
Sickert's late 'Lazarus' self-portraits kill me.
To be reborn into love is to live
a posthumous life. Can you, can anyone,
better the telling?
Shakespeare's Timon not born again into love.

59

Something towers and stoops to its own mind
exactly; it is good merely to sense this.
I am, by my kept word,
a disenfranchised stranger. Strange that my fathers
thought they were not. There goes a fox
like a swift perfect image of itself.
Somewhere a frightened skunk squibs rancid musk.

60

Had intended – what had I not intended?
Praise elemental Job's *ur-Weheklag*,
its iron-cleave, lead-scald? Praise all change
this side of chaos, with the immoveable.
Praise hook-wheeled constellations, praise autumn's
dense clearances, its disfiguring splendours,
far-riding glacial rock, the setting
sun like a stoke-hole, the winter woods
gutted by fire.

61

Stations of the cross are not standard school
crossings, unless for non-standard children.
Not stops on any metro. Some police
barracks may resemble them. Show me
what you are thinking – my *forte*
is melodrama – you are free to go.
Data bases serve also: we are all
made to endure. Made, as in *made*
the Heavens and the Earth, as in *made Man*.

62

Now from sun-stalking rainclouds ‖ that supreme
engine advances, marshalling
familiar cubist layouts, the half-
harvested fields,
blocking their shift-patterns like dazzle
camouflage
on ships in dry dock during the Great War.

63

The city stands to itself, the late
October sky a sportsdome
of clear Fall blue; Virginia creeper,
with ample cladding, warming the brick walls
to a dark glow, a gross finery.
When I close my eyes the sun
beats in silent clamour against them.

64

Time-expired imagination, going down
in wide slow circles, gracefully almost,
like a Fortress over Schweinfurt.
Acquittal here for those no less distinguished,
wound-stripes like velcro scars for him and him.
For her the undead Reichsführer's cryptic doors.
I have made – singularly – a double life
vicarious in parts. Nothing redemptive.
Mouthing aphasias now. Interrogations.

65

Nor is being beside oneself the cue
for revelation, though its arrival stuns:
like the high-piled and brilliantly
toppled bells – their run-of-the-change,
tower-engulfing, average Sunday peal,
a visitation that possesses
foundation and frontage of the shaken air.
Nor is emptiness alone the answer, the tomb
itself open-mouthed.

66

The day, about to be paid off, descends
into its promised ǀ adumbrations
which I do not decline: low-
wattaged fuchsia, far-illuminant,
especially at evening when the sun
draws on its constant yet depleted light,
empowers the sum of innate happiness.

67

With splintering noises the ancient tannoy
celebrates more delay like a bequest
or benefaction long overdue.
An ordinary day, one more rehearsal.
Ducking and weaving, the last flight goes in,
the voice of reason maddens with its fear;
voices of prophecy assail the dead.

68

Again the wind hauls and my yard-tree
shags itself free of leaves. The house rocks
as if to show that it was built on sand.
Very little now ǀ that I do nót
take to be hers in lieu of deprivation:
implausible, credible muse whom I
assuage by night. Unbelievable sex-love,
to which I gave such credence, she believes
our slow corruption by the Song of Songs.

69

The cunning is to swing it, be a hinge
of the unhinged time. At very worst
gaping on all, missing what pillage finds;
at best a portal for the hierarchies.
Something done with – the urge to have begun –
in many ways consigned to be regained.
All on the make, and broken, and exact,
says Milton, England's challenge to Petursson.
In Wintry solstice like the shorten'd light.

70

On mounds of winter city-pigeons flame
drab epaulettes. Clouds over cooling towers
lift and sunder. Call me fantasist
lately assigned to reality. Example
is scansion: instance, to suffer so.
Locate exile | in a basement of field stone
kept by the soughing furnace.

71

First and last, the Denmark Strait takes all
as if by reversion. The Hallgrimskirkja
rears, preternaturally white,
high and dry on its mound, a tribute
to light's pyromania. Everything's
besprent with rayon prisms. The theatre
of obligation offers us refuge.

72

Win some, lose some. The Younger Brother
said Milton should be topped, his books burnt –
this over royalty and the republic:
close to the bone, the resurrection bone
which never could be found though they raked memory
from end to end. And wrought the sarabande,
Sabrina's theme, ascending through the strings
as though such music rounded out mischance.
Dawn-labouring candles twitched their sallow flames.

73

Four days on floor six of the Radisson
Saga ǀ and this had to happen: high density,
high intensity spaces
of imagination. Not much else to observe –
one rotary, three intersections, a school,
a pale house showing the consular flag
of a Scandinavian kingdom. Sketched susurrus
of tyres through slush. The self-flensing ocean
making haphazard signals, idle, urgent.

74

Think of *Tetrachordon*, or, rather, of Milton's
apologetical sonnet, rhetoric
like the exposed
innards of a jumping jack the slightly
salty gunpowder odour.
High-vaunting Hecla, her sulphurious fire –
as in the obscure, curious madrigal.

75

Anytime, now, the final breath-taker,
of which I shall not judge –
not as gravity judges the vortex
or the stone gravity or the targeted
arrow the bow or the magnet
the pendulum, the pendulum mere
misinformalists of time.

76

Got religion, though, down at the heart
of Reykjavik, its little houses,
the old ones rigged like tin Bethels.
I should have bought in
when Iceland went for sale,
settled myself as a famed incógnito,
folk bed, folk table, with a folk
knocker to my door; the yard
dwarf-flowered, the lava summer-hued.

77

Is nothing if not farce
your regular antimasque. But I
have run out of farce and out
of patience with my impatient norseman rôle.
Take it, leave it, the serious work's been done.
Listen! that gnawing sound the big jets make
devouring their flight paths. I'll be out of here
before the first blank ice, well before rotten
gutters grow healthy fangs.

78

Bright cutting-edge or not, I intend to give
notice to my own mind. I suppose
sooner or later we encounter evil
and find little to say.
Remembering though to say:
behind incertitude the vaulting
certitudes I of flume and flame.

79

No, no. Comus screamed like a peacock
at this conclusion. Moral vanity
is his parole, in the off season,
at any time mere sensuality
seems to lie dormant. I know well
the bristling strut, demonic rectitude,
the rod and glass, the masks of his fixation.

80

While the height-challenged sun fades, clouds become
as black-barren as lava, wholly motionless,
not an ashen wisp out of place, while the sun fades.
While the sun fades its fields glow with dark poppies.
Some plenary hand spreads out, to flaunt an end,
old gold imperial colours. Look back a shade –
Guþriþur Þorbjarnardottir – over your
left shoulder or mine ‖ absolute night comes
high-stalking after us.

(3)

A Description of the Antimasque

1

Antimasque, as the Lady said, not anticlimax.
Then let me give you the Laws of Justinian.
Or Petursson's passion-psalms, even more to the point.

I think I shall disguise myself | as an óld mán
and get among the women one last time
in a wolf's pelt of harmlessness, holiness even.

Prophecy is too much, the prophets are too many.
The sea is greenish first, then mustard-yellow,
then chevroned, then broken up,

camouflaged in its abundant colours.
Why do I give you this, why, trembling so,
the meniscus of desire?

2

Sought-after pageantries of light
by darkness annulled; as if by chance
something incomparable gets done; the annulment

blazingly carried through. But now
we are on our own, there is no music.
Ask of me what you will, it is not enough.

Thule's irregular reefs, try naming them
natural pindarics. Our duty is to find
consonance in the disparities, like as not,

duty no less than function – how to rise
to ceremonies of speech; when, why, to address
intrusive suffering.

(57)

3

Antimasque, stiff buffoon! *Sunburning,*
Moonblasting (Milton my friend) the works.
But judge decorum on a sliding scale

itself a float of courtly masquing dances
John Adson would have envied, not to mention
W. and H. Lawes & Co (strange form of words,

that, *not to mention* – it has a name).
The first Comus, Sabrina, were, are, nameless.
What will you give me for yr fifteen minutes

that I would pay myself, or cheat
myself oút of, given half a chance,
granted the delicate footwork of a clown?

4

In patches, profusion – rugosa possibly.
Check out Yule beacons, how they flare, die down,
like giant toaster fires. Seasonal folk-skirlers

with *brennivin* and fiddles muster accordingly,
and with many accordions.
I can't see where, how, resolution applies,

but I am not Hallgrimur Petursson.
If fame is erotic I shall go after fame.
Roses, though, at this latitude?

I mean, when the new year is patently launched,
and metamorphosis absorbs the broached resins;
and when the night's final combustion caps everything.

5

At dense comedic levels fishes probe,
white, flat, luminous, among volcanic
greaves and fissures; find openings

where they nose past the mystic origins
of leprosy and blindness:
Milton's pearl, the *gutta serena*, Hallgrimur

Petursson, his stricken eloquence
all the more to be hailed. Proportionate
disproportion – or equity – it even turns

on this. On this and that, you say. In fact,
you say nothing, god-given Diodati.
Bare preservation is the speaking power.

6

The pulse of the whole fulfils nominal
metronome keepings. Take this as understood.
The narrative's a kind of figured bass,

stark-sounding in the arias. Of crisis
and denial. Sometimes I wish music
meant less to me. Now it's like standing proxy

in a declaration of unanswered love.
Or something like. Sexual
love – what other kind of love ís there,

even for an amorist
of the abstract eros? Hear me
sight-read these as optional cadenzas.

7

Take this one straight from the floor. Do the vigilant
keep the best vigil? Reversed film is not
magnetic force. A rhetorical

question's essential to the dynamic.
Memory of her body is what carries me. Come!
Even though I have no distance to drive.

Mystery means all that's now unobvious
to the inattentive. Axioms
are a dead weight. Or, if you prefer,

they are the tie-rods of argument.
Saved by such rules as these
evoke chaos, chaos that knows its bounds.

8

Image of egg-whites threaded as extruded
through boiling water; Lear's numskull friend
with his tarred whited sockets. *Admit One*

to the theatre, the observatory, to the small
cinema showing new foreign films,
the museum of glances, the Ecclesia

Sancti Pauli in Walton Street.
I had forgotten how the ill-omened road
configures at this point. I catch my breath.

The clue's in the projector, out of focus
for fifty years: a face blurred to declare
itself in some way, some way of saying no.

9

Combative in theory, I hate drawing
my own blood. Blood-line's a different issue,
Severn-side blacksmiths and nailers who must have bled:

I vouch for these, on half-familiar terms.
Ungrateful though they máy be for my voice.
Hallgrimur Petursson's closer to them –

although not in Icelandic. I've yet to find
a well-working translation. Petursson found
that he had leprosy. Segregation works.

The English class system works in its own way.
Neither segregation nor assimilation.
Things won't change though there ís the Euro.

10

Price to be paid in what some stoop to call
grave and sensuous beauty.
I've paid for first refusal, fist over hand.

Rage is impoverishment, spirituality
more like a lead cosmetic [pronounce lɛd].
I was not at my best when I wrote that;

the lines of age too evident. True enough
we are all poisonous to ourselves. Rephrase,
say, áll-manner-wounded by calamity

since what divides us ís incomprehension,
unifier of this swaying, weeping, crowd
hooked to the Freedom-statue's iron birds.

11

Winner arrested, still with gold watch in his
possession. That's something líke a nightmare.
Sleeping without the sleepmask brings it on.

Try Chaucer's mask: the broad way of the wheel,
the public ruin and the private gain;
no-hope encounters with the witch herself,

Circe or Lilith or Lady Mede;
the living fetish of the murdered love;
the rigid fantasist bowed as if for prayer;

the ultimate fixity of things let slide,
the treaty sealed, the treacheries undisclosed;
disclosed, the voyeur's mirror in the wall.

12

So let there be nothing where it stood,
Ludlow's brief mirage: Comus' spectral
body as its material – which might

absently have been conjured. This in worn
September, through Michaelmas. You'd expect
no late miraculous quicksilver in those

quick-falling days. Here's Michaelmas once more:
The sainted angels bearing themselves aloof,
pre-emptive. At Coventry, Epstein's fiercely

applauded Michael sentinels his gaze.
The spire positioned in a vacant lot
soars and is held, alight with the dull rain.

(62)

13

Joy is the full sun and the half shadow.
Twelve sounds unbalanced, no doubt of that –
blasted city fathers! But imbalance

is everywhere. In the tectonic plates
ripping Iceland apart, to cite you basics.
I'm no *Fortuna*-type, though, much as I love

Boethius. And irony has its limits.
If this were adjudged Senecan I'd be honoured.
Surrey's bitter proud jousting, his straight-up

elegy for Wyatt, I can find strength in,
ironic or not. Nót | all óther thíngs
being equal. They áren't and never wíll be.

14

Comus Investments: I have shares in that
ongoing concern. *Ailing Self-Assurance*
dredges a dividend. My antimasque

can afford a vengeance! Voices from the wings
interpolate a chorus. Style for style
Purcell could do me justice, Jonson's words,

or Dryden's, offer satisfaction. Now
the counterpoise. So poise it and retire
into the work. Music of false relation,

solemn music and dance, befitting language
drawn with a difficult mastery of the kinds.
History on call, posterity in rehearsal.

15

Error-heavy work, to be set right
by final showdown. Say, vision and the Fall
use me to sing. Or, idiot-alibi.

From the outset I something of mine failed
the long addition, short détente, between
private and public, purpose, desire, hope.

I was off sick while freedom bells were rung
in three-parts-ruined cities for an age.
Bring back the *Trümmerfrauen*, rubble-women.

I want start-over with a different voice.
Few souls are solitary through force of will.
Here there's no crossing-point from zone to zone.

16

Rilke could read Bible in bad light
or shaky script. Most of what I claim
can be so read. This is a summary

as it is a summons. Though not on oath
repeat after me *the interminable
journey to closure*. Here's a beginning

beginning at the end. For a start it was
not interminable: not since we knew ourselves
appropriately immortal. There was joy –

the unbroken immanence to which I speak –
that day at Stratford, chased by angry swans!
Half-recalled abjurations yet to come.

17

For some cause or other the block stands.
It's like a monument to a mythic poet.
Better, to the commander of a rearguard.

Whether of stone or bronze it is found fractured
if not by vandals by some intrinsic flaw
proper to originality and the medium,

material witness to a state of things
in which our freedom is a type of fate
within the shifting bounds predictable.

A certain way: interpret, sober fear
sprung of a certain knowledge of the odds.
Interpret, crazy shouting on the heath.

18

The reefs of which I spoke: the breakers there
pile with such force you feel their breath expelled
in hearing it. Expelled, never expended,

not off those shores. This is a partial gloss –
I take your challenge. Partiality,
error, relative absolutes

pitching things into shape. Roman theology
hits us with *culpa* – though that's not a coup
except to unwary punsters. Geophysicists

make much of *fault*: fault, with its proper
natural enormity, a geyser's eye
that bulges like the eyeball of a squid.

19

Nothing is unforgettable but guilt.
Guilt of the moment to be made eternal.
Reading immortal literature's a curse.

Beatrice in *The Changeling* makes me sweat
even more than Faustus' Helen, let alone
Marlowe's off-stage blasphemous fun with words

or Pound's last words to silence. Well,
let well alone. The gadgetry of nice
determinism mákes, breáks, comedians.

All the better if you go mad like Pound
(*grillo*, a grasshopper; *grido*, a cry from the fields).
The grief of comedy ǀ you have to laugh.

20

In Wintry solstice like the shorten'd light
sky closes; and sea parts, ranging itself
from unpredicted sources, radiant

when you'd guess blankness under broad shadow.
Hidden artificers ǀ of the visible
withhold what's long been destined to the dark.

In shifting scapes eternity resumes.
I cannot fault its nature, act by act,
gauged by the lost occasions of the sun.

Ephemera's durance, vast particulars
and still momentum measures of the void.
What did you say?